S.H.S.I.C. MINISTRY
Bible Study
The Book of Judith

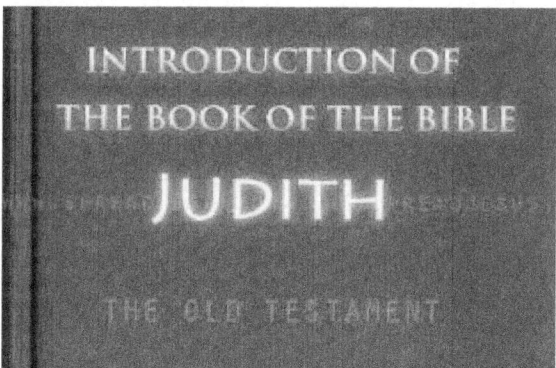

Facilitated by
Karoline Bethea-Jones

Welcome

Welcome to Sisters Helping Sisters in Christ Ministry. My name is Karoline Bethea-Jones and I will be your Ministry leader.

Sisters Helping Sisters in Christ Ministry provides a Christ centered environment where women, young and old, are able to develop and strengthen their walk with Christ, as well as strengthen their relationships within their family and their community

The group promotes spiritual consciousness, and service by encouraging women to serve the needs of their fellow man and the community at large.

I would like to take a moment to welcome you to our ministry and invite you to participate in our lessons.

You can participate in our ministry by signing onto our website, *http://shsicministry.webs.com* and creating a profile.

Our lessons and conference call # will be available if you wish to participate. 1-712-432-0926 Access Code: 1073461.

General Information

Sisters Helping Sisters in Christ Mentoring Ministry is a non-profit organization, which strives to develop a strong fellowship among the young women of our community, with the older women of our churches, for the purpose of strengthening our spiritual walk, and living a life that is pleasing to God.

It is my desire to use this program to encourage, uplift and educate young women who desire to dedicate their lives to Christ, and find it difficult to do so in these troubling times.

In this constantly changing world, the ability to walk alongside others, sharing wisdom and life experiences is an asset.

We learn from each other. We encourage each other. As you mentor, teach, and pray, you see new possibilities and the power of the Holy Spirit at work.

As we follow Jesus' example of mentoring, we in turn will influence those that Christ has given us to disciple. As a role model for others, you know that you are being observed, and that forces you to try to do your best.

You strive to practice what you preach, and this pushes you to try harder.

It is a great way to stay motivated! Mentoring other Christians help to sharpen your own walk with Christ.

THE BOOK OF JUDITH

The Book of Judith relates the story of God's deliverance of the Jewish people. This was accomplished "by the hand of a female"—a constant motif (cf. 8:33; 9:9, 10; 12:4; 13:4, 14, 15; 15:10; 16:5) meant to recall the "hand" of God in the Exodus narrative (cf. Ex 15:6). The work may have been written around 100 B.C., but its historical range is extraordinary. Within the reign of Nebuchadnezzar (1:1; 2:1), it telescopes five centuries of historical and geographical information with imaginary details.

There are references to Nineveh, the Assyrian capital destroyed in 612 B.C., to Nebuchadnezzar, the ruler not of Assyria but of Babylon (605/604-562), and to the second Temple, built around 515. The postexilic period is presumed (e.g., governance by the High Priest).

The Persian period is represented by two characters, Holofernes and Bagoas, who appear together in the military campaigns of Artaxerxes III Ochus (358-338); there seem to be allusions to the second-century Seleucid ruler Antiochus IV Epiphanes. Several mysteries remain: Judith herself, Arphaxad, and others are otherwise unknown.

The geographical details, such as the narrow defile into Bethulia (an unidentified town which gives access to the heart of the land), are fanciful. The simple conclusion from these and other details is that the work is historical fiction, written to exalt God as Israel's deliverer from foreign might, not by an army, but by means of a simple widow.

There are four Greek recensions of Judith (Septuagint codices Vaticanus, Sinaiticus, Alexandrinus, and Basiliano-Vaticanus), four ancient translations (Old Latin, Syriac, Sahidic, and Ethiopic), and some late Hebrew versions, apparently translated from the Vulgate. Despite Jerome's claim to have translated an Aramaic text, no ancient Aramaic or Hebrew manuscripts have been found.

The oldest extant text of Judith is the preservation of 15:1-7 inscribed on a third-century A.D. potsherd. Whatever the reasons, the rabbis did not count Judith among their scriptures, and the Reformation adopted that position. The early Church, however, held this book in high honor. The first-century Pope, St. Clement of Rome, proposes Judith as an example of courageous love (1 Corinthians 55).

St. Jerome holds her up as an example of a holy widow and a type of the Church (To Salvina: Letter 79, par. 10; see also To Furia: Letter 54, par. 16) and, in another place, describes Mary as a new Judith (To Eustochium: Letter 22, par. 21). The Council of Trent

(1546) included Judith in the canon; thus it is one of the seven deuterocanonical books.

Inner-biblical references are noteworthy: as God acted through Moses' hand (Ex 10:21-22; 14:27-30), so God delivers "by the hand of a female," Judith. Like Jael, who drove a tent peg through the head of Sisera (Jgs 4), Judith kills an enemy general. Like Deborah (Jgs 4-5), Judith "judges" Israel in the time of military crisis. Like Sarah, the mother of Israel's future (Gn 17:6), Judith's beauty deceives foreigners, with the result that blessings redound to Israel (Gn 12:11-20).

Her Hebrew name means "Jewish woman." Her exploits captured the imagination of liturgists, artists, and writers through the centuries. The book is filled with double entendres and ironic situations, e.g., Judith's conversation with Holofernes in 11:5-8, 19, where "my lord" is ambiguous, and her declaration to Holofernes that she will lead him through Judea to Jerusalem (his head goes on such a journey).

The book can be divided into five parts:
Assyrian Threat (1:1-3:10)
Siege of Bethulia (4:1-7:32)
Judith, Instrument of the Lord (8:1-10:10)
Judith Goes Out to War (10:11-13:20)
Victory and Thanksgiving (14:1-16:25)

Judith 1

The War between Nebuchadnezzar and Arphaxad

1 While King Nebuchadnezzar was ruling over the Assyrians from his capital city of Nineveh, King Arphaxad ruled over the Medes from his capital city of Ecbatana. ² Around Ecbatana King Arphaxad built a wall 105 feet high and 75 feet thick of cut stones; each stone was 4 1/2 feet thick and 9 feet long. ³ At each gate he built a tower 150 feet high, with a foundation 90 feet thick. ⁴ Each gateway was 105 feet high and 60 feet wide—wide enough for his whole army to march through, with the infantry in formation.

⁵ In the twelfth year of his reign King Nebuchadnezzar went to war against King Arphaxad in the large plain around the city of Rages. ⁶ Many nations joined forces with King Arphaxad—all the people who lived in the mountains, those who lived along the Tigris, Euphrates, and Hydaspes rivers, as well as those who lived in the plain ruled by King Arioch of Elam. Many nations joined this Chelodite alliance.

⁷ Then King Nebuchadnezzar of Assyria sent a message to the Persians and to the people to the west, in the regions of Cilicia, Damascus, Lebanon, Antilebanon, to those along the coast, ⁸ and in the regions of Carmel,

Gilead, northern Galilee, and Jezreel Valley. 9-10 The message also went to the people living in Samaria and the nearby towns, to those in the area west of the Jordan River as far as the cities of Jerusalem, Bethany, Chelous, and Kadesh, and to the district of Goshen. The message was also taken to the Egyptian cities of Tahpanhes, Rameses, Tanis, and Memphis, and the district up the Nile River to the Ethiopian[a] border. 11 But everyone in this whole region ignored King Nebuchadnezzar's appeal and refused to take part in the war. They thought that he had no chance of winning the war, so they were not afraid of him and sent his messengers back disgraced and empty-handed.

12 This made Nebuchadnezzar so furious that he vowed he would risk his entire kingdom to take revenge on all those people. He vowed that he would put to death the entire population of Cilicia, Damascus, Syria, Moab, Ammon, Judah, and Egypt—everyone from the Mediterranean Sea to the Persian Gulf.

13 In the seventeenth year of his reign King Nebuchadnezzar led his army into battle against King Arphaxad. He defeated all of Arphaxad's forces, including his entire cavalry, and all his charioteers. 14 Then Nebuchadnezzar occupied all the towns in the land of Media and advanced against the city of Ecbatana. He captured the city's towers, looted its markets, and

made that beautiful city a ruin. [15] He captured King Arphaxad in the mountains around Rages and killed him. After Arphaxad's death, [16] Nebuchadnezzar and his entire army returned to Nineveh with all the loot taken in battle. There they relaxed and feasted for four months.

Judith 2

The War against the Nations in the West

2 In the eighteenth year of Nebuchadnezzar's reign, on the twenty-second day of the first month of that year, he and his advisers decided to carry out his threat to take revenge on all those countries that had refused to help him. ²⁻³ The king called his general staff and senior officers together and reported in detail how those countries had betrayed him. He and his officers agreed that everyone who had refused to help him in the war should be put to death. Then he described to them his plan of attack.

⁴ At the close of the meeting, Nebuchadnezzar gave the following command to Holofernes, who was the general in command of his armies and second in command to the king:

⁵   I, Nebuchadnezzar, the great king and ruler of all the earth, command you to choose some experienced soldiers: 120,000 infantry and 12,000 cavalry. ⁶ Then attack the lands to the west because they refused to respond to my appeal for help. ⁷ Warn them that they must prepare their offerings of earth and water to show that they have surrendered unconditionally. I will make them feel the full force of my anger and completely

destroy them. My armies will march over every foot of their land and plunder it as they go. 8 I will fill the valleys with their dead bodies and will choke up every stream and river with so many corpses that they will all overflow. 9 I will take captive all those who are left alive and carry them off to the ends of the earth.

10 But you, Holofernes, are ordered to go ahead of me and occupy all their territories in advance. If they surrender to you, hold them for me until I come to punish them. 11 But if they resist, do not spare them. Kill them and loot the entire region under your control. 12 I have taken a solemn vow, and at the risk of my life and my royal power I am determined to do what I have vowed to do.13 Do not disobey me in any way. I am your king; remember that, and carry out without delay every order that I have given you.

The Campaign of Holofernes

14 So Holofernes left the king and called together all the commanders, generals, and officers of the Assyrian army. 15 Just as the king had ordered, he chose 120,000 of the best infantrymen and 12,000 of the best mounted archers16 and arranged them in battle formation. 17 He also took along a very large number of camels, donkeys, and mules to carry the equipment, as well as many sheep, cattle, and goats for food. 18 Every soldier

received plenty of rations and a large payment of gold and silver from the royal treasury.

19 Then Holofernes and his entire army set out, advancing ahead of King Nebuchadnezzar. The chariots, the cavalry, and the infantry marched out to overrun the entire western region. 20 Other troops went with them. There were so many that it was impossible to count them—they were like a swarm of locusts or like grains of sand in the desert.

21 Three days after they had left the city of Nineveh, they reached the plains around Bectileth near the mountains north of Cilicia, where they set up camp.22 From there Holofernes advanced into the hill country with his entire army, his infantry, cavalry, and chariots. 23 He totally destroyed the countries of Libya and Lydia, then plundered all the people of Rassis and the Ishmaelites who lived on the edge of the desert, south of the land of the Chelleans.

24 Then Holofernes crossed the Euphrates River and marched through the land of Mesopotamia, completely destroying all the walled towns along the Abron River as far as the sea. 25 He seized the territory of Cilicia, killing everyone who resisted him, and went as far as the southern borders of the land of Japheth, near Arabia. 26 He surrounded the Midianites, burned down their tents, and slaughtered their sheep.

27 Holofernes went down into the plains around Damascus during the wheat harvest, burned all the fields, slaughtered the flocks and herds, looted the towns, devastated the entire countryside, and killed all the young men. 28 Panic seized all the people who lived along the Mediterranean Sea, and they shook with fear. Everyone in the towns of Tyre, Sidon, Sur, Ocina, Jamnia, Ashdod, and Ashkelon was terrified.

Judith 3

The Peace Delegation to King Nebuchadnezzar

3 All these nations sent a peace delegation to King Nebuchadnezzar with this message:

2 We remain loyal to you, great King Nebuchadnezzar; we are ready to serve you and obey any command that you may wish to give us. ³ Our buildings, all our land, our wheat fields, our livestock, and our tents are at your disposal; use them in any way you wish. ⁴ Our people will be your slaves, and you may use our towns as you please.

⁵ After the peace delegation had brought this message, ⁶ Holofernes led Nebuchadnezzar's army down to the Mediterranean coast. He stationed guards in all the walled towns and selected certain local men in each of the towns as reserve troops. ⁷ The people in the towns and in the surrounding countryside welcomed Holofernes by wearing wreaths of flowers and dancing to the beat of drums. ⁸ But Holofernes destroyed all their places of worship[a] and cut down their sacred trees. He had been ordered to destroy all the gods of the land so that all the nations and tribes would worship only Nebuchadnezzar and pray to him as a god.

⁹ Then Holofernes passed through Jezreel Valley near Dothan, which faces the main ridge of the mountains of Judah, ¹⁰ and set up camp between Geba and Scythopolis. He stayed there for a month in order to get supplies for his army.

Judith 4

The Israelite Plan for Defense

4 The people of Judah heard what Holofernes, the commander of King Nebuchadnezzar's armies, had done to the other nations. They heard how he had looted and destroyed all their temples, ² and they were terrified of him and afraid of what he might do to Jerusalem and to the Temple of the Lord their God. ³ They had only recently returned home to Judah from exile and had just rededicated the Temple and its utensils and its altar after they had been defiled. ⁴ So they sent a warning to the whole region of Samaria and to the towns of Kona, Beth Horon, Belmain, Jericho, Choba, and Aesora, and to Salem Valley. ⁵ They immediately occupied the mountaintops, fortified the villages on the mountains, and stored up food in preparation for war. It was fortunate that they had recently harvested their fields.

⁶ The High Priest Joakim, who was in Jerusalem at that time, wrote to the people in the towns of Bethulia and Betomesthaim, which face Jezreel Valley near Dothan. ⁷ He ordered them to occupy the mountain passes which led into the land of Judah, where it would be easy to withstand an attack, since the approach was only wide enough for two people at a time to pass. ⁸ The

Israelites carried out the orders given to them by the High Priest Joakim and the Council which met in Jerusalem.

Prayer before the War

[9] The leaders of Israel prayed earnestly to God and fasted. [10] They put on sackcloth—they and their wives, their children, their livestock, and every resident foreigner, every slave and hired laborer. [11-12] They also covered the altar with sackcloth. Then all the men, women, and children in Jerusalem lay face down on the ground in front of the Temple; they lay there in the Lord's presence, all in sackcloth, their heads covered with ashes.

They joined together in earnest prayer to the God of Israel, begging him not to let their children be captured, their wives carried off, or their home towns destroyed. They pleaded with him not to give the Gentiles the satisfaction of destroying the Temple and dishonoring it. [13] [a]The Lord heard their prayers and saw their distress. For many days the people of Judah and Jerusalem continued their fast in front of the Temple of the Lord Almighty. [14]

The High Priest Joakim, the priests, and all the others who served in the Lord's Temple, wore sackcloth when they offered the daily burnt offering, the freewill offerings of the people, and the offerings made to fulfill a vow. [15] They put ashes on their turbans and cried out in prayer to the Lord, begging him to have mercy on the whole nation.

Judith 5

The War Council in the Camp of Holofernes

5 When Holofernes, the Assyrian general, heard that the Israelites had prepared for war, blocked the mountain passes, fortified the mountaintops, and set up roadblocks in the plains, [2] he boiled over with anger. He called together all the Moabite rulers, all the Ammonite generals, and all the governors of the region along the Mediterranean coast [3] and said to them,

You live in Canaan, so tell me about the people who live in these mountains. Which cities do they occupy? How large is their army? What is the source of their power and strength? Who is the king who leads their army? [4] Why have they alone, of all the people in the west, refused to come out and surrender to me?

The Speech of Achior

[5] Then Achior, the leader of all the Ammonites, answered Holofernes,

Sir, if you will please be so kind as to listen to me, I will tell you the truth about these people who live in the mountains near your camp. I will not lie to you. [6] These people are the descendants of some Babylonians [7-8] who abandoned the ways of their ancestors in order to worship the God of heaven. Finally, they were driven out of their land because they refused to worship their ancestors' gods. Then they fled to Mesopotamia, where they settled and lived for a long time.

[9] Afterward, their god told them to leave Mesopotamia and go to the land of Canaan, where they settled and became very rich in gold, silver, and livestock.[10] Later, when a famine struck all the land of Canaan, these Israelites, as they were later called, went down to Egypt and stayed there as long as there was enough food. While they were there, they became a large nation with so many people that they could not be counted.

[11] So the king of Egypt turned against them. He took advantage of them and put them to work making bricks. He oppressed them and made them slaves. [12] But they prayed to their god, and he sent disasters that left the Egyptians helpless. When the Egyptians drove them out of the country, [13] their god dried up the Red Sea in front of them, [14] and then led them along the way to Sinai and Kadesh Barnea.

The Israelites drove out all the people who lived in the southern part of Canaan, [15] occupied the land of the Amorites, wiped out the people of Heshbon, crossed the Jordan River, and took possession of the entire mountain region.[16] They drove out the Canaanites, the Perizzites, the Jebusites, the Shechemites, and all the Girgashites.

The Israelites have now lived in these mountains for a long time.

¹⁷ Their god hates wickedness, and as long as they did not sin against him, they prospered. ¹⁸ But when they disobeyed him, they suffered heavy losses in many wars and were finally taken away as captives to a foreign country. The temple of their god was leveled and their cities were occupied by their enemies.

¹⁹ But now that they have returned to their god, they have come back home from the countries where they had been scattered. They have again taken possession of the city of Jerusalem, where their temple is, and have resettled in the mountains that had remained uninhabited.

²⁰ Sir, if these people are now sinning against their god, even unknowingly, and if we can be sure that they are guilty of some offense, we can successfully attack them. ²¹ But if they have not disobeyed the law of their god, then you should leave them alone, or he will defend them, and we will be disgraced before the whole world.

The Reaction of the Crowd

²² When Achior had finished his speech, all the people standing around the tent began to protest. Holofernes' own senior officers, as well as the Moabites and those from the Mediterranean coast, demanded that Achior be put to death.

²³ Why should we be afraid of these Israelites? they asked.

They are weak; they can't put up a strong defense. ²⁴ Let's go ahead! General Holofernes, your great army will slaughter them easily.

Judith 6

The Speech of Holofernes

6 When the noise of the crowd around the council had subsided, Holofernes spoke to Achior in front of the entire group, those from the Mediterranean coast, the Moabites, and the Ammonite mercenaries.[a]

2 Achior,[b] who do you think you are, acting like a prophet? Who are you to tell us not to go to war against the Israelites because some god will defend them? Nebuchadnezzar is our god, and that's all that matters. He will send his army and wipe these Israelites off the face of the earth. Their god can't help them. 3 But we serve Nebuchadnezzar, and we will beat them as easily as if their whole army were one man.

They will not be able to hold their ground against our cavalry; 4 it will overwhelm them. The mountains will be soaked with their blood, and the valleys will be filled with their corpses. After our attack, they will be completely wiped out; not a trace of them will be left. This is the command of Nebuchadnezzar, the lord of the whole earth, and he doesn't speak idle words.

5 Achior, you are nothing but an Ammonite mercenary, and you talk like a traitor. You will not see me again until I come and punish this race of runaway

slaves. [6] And when I do, my soldiers will put you to death. You will be just another name on the casualty list.

[7] Now my men will take you into the mountains and leave you in one of the Israelite towns, [8] and you will die with the people there. [9] Why look so worried, Achior? Don't you think the town can stand against me? I will carry out all my threats; you can be sure of that!

Achior Is Brought to Bethulia

[10] Then Holofernes ordered his men, who were waiting in his tent, to seize Achior, take him to Bethulia, and hand him over to the Israelites. [11] So the men seized Achior and took him out of the camp into the valley. From there they led him into the mountains, as far as the spring which was below Bethulia.

[12] When the men of that town saw them approaching, they picked up their weapons and ran to the top of the hill. Every man who used a sling as a weapon rained stones down on Holofernes' soldiers, and this stopped them from coming any farther up the mountain. [13] The Assyrians were forced to take cover along the mountainside, where they tied Achior up and left him lying at the foot of the mountain. Then they returned to Holofernes.

[14] Later, when the Israelites came down from Bethulia, they untied Achior, brought him into the town, and took him before the town officials, [15] who at that

time were Uzziah son of Micah, of the tribe of Simeon, Chabris son of Gothoniel, and Charmis son of Melchiel. [16] The officials called together the town elders, and all the women and the young men also ran to the assembly. Achior was brought before the people, and Uzziah began questioning him. [17] Achior told them what had been said at Holofernes' war council, what he himself had said to the Assyrian officers, and how Holofernes had boasted about what he would do to the Israelites. [18] When the people heard this, they fell on their knees and worshiped God. They prayed:

[19] O Lord God of heaven, look how our boastful enemies have humiliated your people! Have pity on us and help us. [20] Then they reassured Achior and praised him for what he had done. [21] After the assembly was over, Uzziah took Achior home with him, and gave a banquet there for the elders. All that night they prayed to the God of Israel for help.

Judith 7

The Siege of Bethulia

¹⁻² The next day Holofernes gathered his whole army together, as well as his allied forces. It was an immense army, consisting of 170,000 infantry and 12,000 cavalry, not counting the support troops who took care of the equipment. He ordered them to march on Bethulia, seize the mountain passes, and attack the Israelites. So they moved out ³ and set up camp beside the spring in the valley near Bethulia. The camp was so wide that it spread out toward the town of Dothan as far as Balbaim, and so long that it stretched from Bethulia to Cyamon, which faces Jezreel Valley.

⁴ When the Israelites saw the size of the army, they were terrified and said to one another,

Those soldiers are going to eat up everything in sight. There's not enough food in the mountains, valleys, and hills put together to feed an army like that. ⁵ But in spite of their fear, all the Israelites took up their weapons, lighted signal fires on the towers, and remained on guard duty all night. ⁶ The next day Holofernes led out his entire cavalry so that the Israelites in Bethulia could see them. ⁷ He inspected the approaches to the town and the springs that supplied its water. He seized the springs and stationed guards there, before returning to camp.

8 All the leaders of the Edomite and Moabite forces, along with the commanders of the troops from the Mediterranean coast, came to Holofernes and said, 9 Sir, if you listen to our advice, your troops will not suffer heavy losses. 10 These Israelites do not rely on their weapons for defense but rather on the height of the mountains where they live, since the mountains are not easy to climb.

11 So then, General Holofernes, if you do not make a direct attack on them, your whole army will suffer no casualties. 12 Stay in your camp and keep your soldiers in their quarters. Just command your men to blockade the springs at the foot of the mountains, 13 because that's where the people of Bethulia come to draw their water. Then, when they are dying of thirst, they will surrender their town to you. Meanwhile, we and our men will go up to the tops of the surrounding mountains, where we will set up camp and keep anyone from leaving the town.

14 Everyone will starve to death—men, women, and children. Even before we attack, the streets will be littered with their corpses. 15 In this way you can make them pay for their rebellion and for refusing to surrender peacefully to you.

¹⁶ Holofernes and his entire staff were pleased with this suggestion, so he gave orders to put the plan into action. ¹⁷ The Moabites and 5,000 Assyrians moved their camp into the valley to control the source of the town's water. ¹⁸ The Edomites and the Ammonites went up into the mountains and set up their camp opposite the town of Dothan. They sent some of their men to the southeast in the direction of Acraba, near Chusi, which is beside the Mochmur River. The rest of the Assyrian army set up camp in the valley. Their camp was spread out over the whole countryside, because the number of tents and the amount of equipment needed for such a large army were immense.

¹⁹ Then the Israelites cried out to the Lord their God for help. They had lost their courage, for with the enemy all around them there was no way to escape.²⁰ The entire Assyrian army—infantry, chariots, and cavalry—blockaded Bethulia for thirty-four days until the town ran out of water. ²¹ All the reservoirs and cisterns went dry, so that the drinking water had to be rationed, and not a day passed when there was enough water to go around. ²² Children were becoming weak; everywhere throughout the town women and young people were collapsing. No one had any strength left.

²³ All the people of the town—men, women, and children alike—gathered around Uzziah and the town

officials and shouted in protest,

24   God will punish you for what you have done to us! You are to blame for what is happening, because you did not make peace with the Assyrians. 25 There is no one to help us now! God has put us in their power. We are exhausted and dying of thirst. 26 Call the Assyrians now and surrender to them, and let Holofernes and his army take the town and loot it. 27 We are better off as prisoners of war. They will make us slaves, but at least we will be alive, and we won't have to watch our wives and children dying before our eyes. 28 Heaven and earth are witnesses against you, and so is our God, the Lord of our ancestors, who is punishing us for their sins as well as ours. We can only hope and pray that he will not let these terrible things happen to us today.

[a]

29 Everyone there began to weep loudly and to pray to the Lord their God. 30 Then Uzziah said to them,

Don't give up, my friends! Let's wait five more days to see if the Lord our God will be merciful to us. Surely he will not abandon us completely. 31 But if no help comes after five days, then I will do as you say.

32 So Uzziah dismissed the people. All the men returned to their guard posts on the walls and towers, while the women and children went back to their homes.

The morale of the entire town was very low.

30

Judith 8

Judith, the Israelite Widow

8 At that time, Judith heard about Uzziah's decision. She was the daughter of Merari, the granddaughter of Ox and the great-granddaughter of Joseph. Joseph's ancestors were Oziel, Elkiah, Ananias, Gideon, Raphaim, Ahitub, Elijah, Hilkiah, Eliab, Nathanael, Salamiel, Sarasadai, and Israel. ² Judith's husband Manasseh, who belonged to the same tribe and clan, had died during the barley harvest. ³ He had suffered a sunstroke while in the fields supervising the farm workers and later died in bed at home in Bethulia. He was buried in the family tomb in the field between Dothan and Balamon.

⁴ For three years and four months, Judith had lived as a widow. ⁵ In her grief she built a little shelter on the roof of her house and lived there, wearing sackcloth. ⁶ She fasted during that entire period except when fasting was forbidden: the day before the Sabbath and the Sabbath itself, the eve of the New Moon Festival and the Festival itself, and all the festivals and holidays observed by the people of Israel. ⁷ Judith was a very beautiful woman. Her husband had left her gold and silver, servants and slaves, livestock and fields. She continued to supervise the

estate, [8] and no one ever said anything bad about Judith. She was a very religious woman.

Judith Meets with the Town Officials

[9] Judith heard how the people were complaining bitterly against Uzziah, now that the water shortage had broken their morale. She learned that in answer to their complaints he had promised to surrender the town to the Assyrians after five days. [10] Judith sent a slave, the woman who managed her business affairs, to invite Uzziah,[a] Chabris, and Charmis, the town officials, to her home.

[11] When the officials arrived, Judith said to them,

Please listen to me. You are the leaders of the people of Bethulia, but you were wrong to speak to the people as you did today. You should not have made a solemn promise before God that you would surrender the town to our enemies if the Lord did not come to our aid within a few days. [12] What right do you have to put God to the test as you have done today? Who are you to put yourselves in God's place in dealing with human affairs?

[13] It is the Lord Almighty that you are putting to the test! Will you never learn? [14] There is no way that you can understand what is in the depths of a human heart or find out what a person is thinking. Yet you dare to read God's mind and interpret his thoughts! How can you claim to

understand God, the Creator? No, my friends, you must stop arousing the anger of the Lord our God! ¹⁵ If he decides not to come to our aid within five days, he still may rescue us at any time he chooses. Or he may let our enemies destroy us. ¹⁶ But you must not lay down conditions for the Lord our God! Do you think that he is like one of us? Do you think you can bargain with him or force him to make a decision?¹⁷ No! Instead, we should ask God for his help and wait patiently for him to rescue us. If he wants to, he will answer our cry for help.

¹⁸ We do not worship gods made with human hands. Not one of our clans, tribes, towns, or cities has ever done that, even though our ancestors used to do so. ¹⁹ That is why God let their enemies kill them and take everything they had. It was a great defeat! ²⁰ But since we worship no other God but the Lord, we can hope that he will not reject us or any of our people.

²¹ If our town is taken by the enemy, the entire region of Judah will then fall, and our Temple in Jerusalem will be looted. And God will make us pay with our lives for allowing the Temple to be defiled. ²² He will hold us responsible for the slaughter and captivity of our people and for the destruction of the land we have inherited. We will be despised and mocked by the people in those nations to which we will be taken as slaves. ²³ We are not going to win the favor of our enemies by surrendering

to them now.[b] If we do surrender, the Lord our God will see that we are put to shame.

24 No, my friends, we should set an example for our own people. Not only their lives, but the fate of the Temple and the altar depend on us. 25 The Lord our God is putting us to the test, just as he tested our ancestors, and we should be thankful for that. 26 Remember how he put Abraham and Isaac to the test, and what happened to Jacob while he was working as a shepherd for his uncle Laban in Mesopotamia. 27 God is not testing our loyalty as severely as he did theirs. God is not sending this punishment on us as revenge, but as a warning to us who worship him.

28 Then Uzziah answered Judith,

Everything you have said makes good sense, and no one can argue with it. 29 This is not the first time you have shown wisdom. Ever since you were a child, all of us have recognized the soundness and maturity of your judgment. 30 But our people are dying of thirst. They forced us to say what we did and to make a solemn promise, which we cannot break.31 So now, since you are a deeply religious woman, pray for our people; ask the Lord to send rain to fill our cisterns, so that we can get our strength back.

32 All right, Judith replied,

I am going to do something which our Jewish people

will never forget.[33] Tonight, the three of you must stand guard at the gate so that my slave woman and I can leave the town. And before the day comes on which you have promised to surrender, the Lord will use me to rescue the people of Israel. [34] But you must not ask me what I am going to do; I will explain it to you when it is all over.

[35] Uzziah and the other officials said to her,

You have our blessing. May the Lord our God guide you as you take revenge on our enemies. Then they left Judith's rooftop shelter and returned to their posts.

Judith 9

Judith's Prayer

9 Then Judith put ashes on her head, opened her robe to reveal the sackcloth she was wearing under her clothes, and bowed down with her face to the floor. It was the time that the evening incense was being offered in the Temple in Jerusalem, and Judith prayed in a loud voice: 2

O Lord, the God of my ancestor Simeon, remember how you armed Simeon with a sword to take revenge on those foreigners who seized Dinah, who was a virgin, tore off her clothes,[a] and defiled her; they stripped her naked and shamed her; they raped her and disgraced her, even though you had forbidden this. ³ That is why you let their leaders be killed—put to death on the same bed where they had raped the woman. You destroyed them all, slaves, princes, and rulers on their thrones.⁴ You let their wives be carried off, their daughters taken captive, and their possessions plundered by the Israelites, your chosen people, who were eager to do your will. Dinah's brothers were furious because of this disgrace to their family, so they called on you for help.

O my God, listen to my prayer, the prayer of a widow. ⁵ Your hand guided all that happened then, and all that happened before and after. You have planned it all—

what is happening now, and what is yet to be. Your plans have always been carried out. [6] Whatever you want to be done is as good as done. You know in advance all that you will do and what decisions you will make. [7] Now the Assyrians are stronger than ever; they take pride in their cavalry and their infantry. They rely on their weapons, but they do not know that you, O Lord, are a warrior who ends war. The Lord is your name. [8] In your anger, use your power to shatter their mighty army. They plan to defile your Temple, where you are worshiped, and to hack off the corners of your altar with their swords.[9] Look how proud and boastful they are! Pour out your fury upon them! I am only a widow, but give me the strength to carry out my plan. [10] Use my deceitful words to strike them all dead, master and slave alike. Let a woman's strength break their pride. [11] Your power does not depend on the size and strength of an army. You are a God who cares for the humble and helps the oppressed. You give support and protection to people who are weak and helpless; you save those who have lost hope. [12] Now hear my prayer, O God of my ancestor Simeon, the God in whom Israel trusts, ruler of heaven and earth, creator of the rivers and the seas, king of all creation. Hear my prayer and[13] [c]let my deceitful words wound and kill those who have planned such cruelty against your covenant and your holy Temple, against Mount Zion and the land you have given your people. [14] Make your whole nation and every tribe recognize that you are God, almighty and all-powerful, and that you alone protect the people of Israel!

Judith 10

Judith Goes to the Camp of Holofernes

10 When Judith had finished her prayer to the God of Israel, ² she stood up, called her slave woman, and went down into the house as she always did on Sabbaths and festival days. ³ She took off the sackcloth and her widow's clothes, took a bath, and put on rich perfumes. She brushed her hair, tied a ribbon around it, and dressed herself in the fine clothes she used to wear on joyful occasions when her husband Manasseh was still alive.

⁴ She put on sandals and all her finest jewelry: rings and earrings, and bracelets on her wrists and ankles. She made herself so beautiful that she was sure to attract the attention of any man who saw her. ⁵ Judith gave her slave woman a leather bag of wine and a jar of oil to carry. She filled a bag with roasted barley, cakes of dried figs, and several loaves of bread baked according to Jewish food laws. She carefully wrapped all the food and dishes and gave them to her slave.

⁶ Then the two women left the house and went to the gates of Bethulia, where they found Uzziah and the town officials, Chabris and Charmis, standing guard.⁷ When the men saw Judith after she had changed clothes and

put on make-up, they were struck by her beauty and said to her,

⁸ May the God of our ancestors bless you and make your plan successful, so that you may bring glory to Jerusalem and victory to Israel.

Judith prayed ⁹ and then said,

Order the gates to be opened for me. I am on my way to do what we were talking about. Then they ordered the young men to open the gates for her, ¹⁰ and Judith and her slave left the city. The men watched her as she went down the mountain into the valley, until she was out of sight.

¹¹ As the two women were walking through the valley, an Assyrian patrol met them. ¹² They arrested Judith and questioned her,

What is your nationality? Where did you come from, and where are you going?

I am a Hebrew, she answered, but I am running away from the Israelites because God is going to let you destroy them. ¹³ I am on my way to see Holofernes, the general in command of your army, to give him some reliable information. I can show him how to advance into the mountains and take control of the entire region without a single casualty.

¹⁴ The men stared at her because she was so beautiful. They listened to her story and said,

¹⁵ You have saved your life by coming down here to see our general. Some of us will take you to his headquarters and present you to him. ¹⁶ Do not be afraid of him. Just tell him what you have told us, and he will treat you well.

¹⁷ They assigned a hundred men to escort Judith and her slave to the headquarters of Holofernes.

¹⁸ There was great commotion in the Assyrian camp as news of Judith's arrival spread from tent to tent. While she stood outside the tent of Holofernes waiting to be presented to him, many Assyrian soldiers came and stood around her. ¹⁹ They were greatly impressed by her beauty and wondered what kind of people the Israelites were.

Who can have contempt for people whose women are so beautiful? they asked one another.
We had better kill all the men, or else these Jews will be able to charm the whole world.

²⁰ Then Holofernes' bodyguard and his personal servants came out and led Judith into the tent. ²¹ Holofernes was resting on his bed under a mosquito net woven of purple and gold thread and decorated with emeralds and other precious stones. ²² When the men told him that Judith had arrived, he came to the outer part of the tent. Silver lamps were carried ahead of him. ²³ When Judith came near him

and his servants, they were all astonished at her beauty. She bowed down to the ground before Holofernes, but his servants helped her to her feet.

Judith 11

11 Holofernes said to Judith, "Don't worry; there's no need for you to be afraid. I have never hurt anyone who was willing to serve Nebuchadnezzar, king of the whole world. ² Even now, if your people up in the mountains had not insulted me, I would not have declared war on them. They have brought all this trouble on themselves. ³ But tell me, why have you left them and come to us? You will be safe here. No need to be afraid! We have spared your life tonight, and you are in no danger for the future. ⁴ No one here will harm you; everyone will treat you well, like all other servants of my master, Nebuchadnezzar".

⁵ Then Judith said to Holofernes,

Allow me to speak to you, my lord, and please listen to what I have to say. I will tell you the truth. ⁶ If you follow my advice, God will do something great with you, and my lord will not fail in his plan. ⁷ For I swear to you by the life and strength of Nebuchadnezzar, king of the whole world, who sent you to bring order to all the subjects of his kingdom, that not only have you made people serve him, but because of you even the wild animals, the livestock, and the birds obey him. Because of you, Nebuchadnezzar and his entire kingdom will prosper.

¹⁸ We have heard how wise and clever you are. The whole world knows that you are the most competent,

skilled, and accomplished general in the whole Assyrian Empire. ⁹ Achior was rescued by the men of Bethulia, and has told us what he said at your war council. ¹⁰ Please, sir, do not dismiss lightly what Achior told you, but take it seriously, because it is true. No one can harm or conquer our people unless they sin against their God.

¹¹ But you will not suffer any setbacks, nor will you fail to achieve your goal. When the Israelites sin and make their God angry, they will die. ¹² Their food supply has already run out, and the water shortage has become serious, so they have decided to kill their livestock and eat foods that God's Law clearly forbids them to eat. ¹³ They have decided to eat the wheat set aside from the early harvest and the tithes of wine and oil, which are holy and are reserved for the priests who serve God in Jerusalem. The rest of us are forbidden even to touch this sacred food,

¹⁴ but since the people in Jerusalem have already broken this law, the people of our town have sent messengers to the Council there requesting permission to do the same. ¹⁵ On the day that they receive permission and actually eat the food, you will be able to destroy them. ¹⁶ As soon as I learned about this, I ran away from my people. God has sent me to do something with you that will amaze everyone in the entire world who hears about it. ¹⁷ Sir, I am a religious woman; I worship

the God of heaven day and night. I will stay here in your camp, and each night I will go out into the valley to pray to God, and he will tell me when the Israelites have sinned. [18] As soon as I find out, I will come and tell you, and you can march out with your whole army. The Israelites will not be able to defend themselves against you.

[19] I will guide you through the central part of the land of Judah until we come to Jerusalem, where I will crown you king in the center of the city. You will scatter the people of Jerusalem like sheep without a shepherd. Not even a dog will dare to growl at you. God has revealed these things to me in advance and has sent me to report them to you.

[20] Holofernes and his personal servants were pleased with what Judith had said, and they admired her wisdom. [21] She must be the wisest and most beautiful woman in the world, they commented one to another.

[22] Then Holofernes said to her,

It's a good thing that God has sent you here to bring us victory and to destroy those who have insulted King Nebuchadnezzar. [23] Not only are you beautiful, but you know how to make a speech. If you do as you have promised, your God will be my God. You will live in King Nebuchadnezzar's palace and will be famous throughout the world.

Judith 12

Judith Remains Faithful to Her Religion

12 Holofernes commanded his men to take Judith to the table which was set with his silverware and to serve her some of his own special food and wine.² But Judith refused.

I cannot eat your food, she said,
for I would be breaking the laws of my God. I will eat only what I have brought with me.

³ But what will you do when your food and wine are gone? Holofernes asked.
Where will we get more food for you? There are no Israelites here in our camp.

⁴ Sir, Judith answered,
as surely as you live, I have more than enough food to last until the Lord has used me to carry out his plan.

⁵ Then Holofernes' personal servants led Judith to a tent. She slept there until the time of the morning watch just before dawn, when she got up ⁶ and sent a message to Holofernes requesting permission to go out into the valley to pray.⁷ Holofernes ordered his guards to let Judith leave the camp. So for three days Judith lived in the camp, and each night she would go out to the valley near Bethulia and bathe at the spring. ⁸ After she had bathed,

she would pray to the Lord God to guide her in her plan to bring victory to Israel. [9] Then she would return to the camp ritually pure and remain in her tent until after the evening meal.

Holofernes' Banquet

[10] On the fourth day of Judith's stay in the camp, Holofernes gave a banquet for his highest ranking officers, but he did not invite any of the officers who were on duty. [11] He said to Bagoas, the eunuch who was in charge of his personal affairs,

Go and persuade the Hebrew woman, who is in your care, to come to my tent to eat and drink with us. [12] It would be a shame to pass up an opportunity to make love to a woman like that. If I don't try to seduce her, she will laugh at me.

[13] So Bagoas left Holofernes and went to Judith.

Lovely lady, he said,

the general invites you to his tent for some drinks. Come and enjoy yourself like the Assyrian women who serve in Nebuchadnezzar's palace. This is a great honor.

[14] I shall be glad to accept, Judith answered. How could I refuse? I'll remember this happy night as long as I live.

[15] So Judith got up and put on her prettiest clothes. Her slave woman went ahead of her and placed on the ground in front of Holofernes the lamb skins that

Bagoas had given Judith to sit on when she ate. [16] Judith came into the tent and sat down there. Holofernes was aroused when he saw her and had an uncontrollable desire to make love to her. From the first day he had seen her, he had been waiting for a chance to seduce her.

[17] Join us for a drink and enjoy yourself, he said to her.

[18] I'll be glad to, sir, Judith replied; this is the happiest day of my life. [19] But even then Judith ate and drank only what her slave had prepared. [20] Holofernes was so charmed by her that he drank more wine than he had ever drunk at one time in his whole life.

Judith 13

13 Finally, when it got late, the guests excused themselves and left. Bagoas then closed up the tent from the outside and prevented Holofernes' servants from going in. So they all went to bed; everyone was very tired because the banquet had lasted so long. ² Judith was left alone in the tent with Holofernes who was lying drunk on his bed. ³ Judith's slave woman was waiting outside the tent for Judith to go and pray, as she had done each night. Judith had also told Bagoas that she would be going out to pray as usual.

⁴ All the guests and servants were now gone, and Judith and Holofernes were alone in the tent. Judith stood by Holofernes' bed and prayed silently,

O Lord, God Almighty, help me with what I am about to do for the glory of Jerusalem. ⁵ Now is the time to rescue your chosen people and to help me carry out my plan to destroy the enemies who are threatening us.

⁶ Judith went to the bedpost by Holofernes' head and took down his sword.⁷ She came closer, seized Holofernes by the hair of his head, and said,

O Lord, God of Israel, give me strength now. ⁸ Then Judith raised the sword and struck him twice in the neck as hard as she could, chopping off his head. ⁹ She rolled his body off the bed and took down the mosquito net from the bedposts. Then she came out and gave Holofernes' head to her slave, [10] who put it in the food bag.

Judith and Her Slave Return to Bethulia

Then the two women left together, as they always did when they went to pray. After they had walked through the Assyrian camp, they crossed the valley and went up the mountainside until they came to the gates of Bethulia. [11] When they were a short distance away, Judith called out to the guards at the gate,

Open the gate! Open the gate! Our God is still with us. Today he has once again shown his strength in Israel and used his power against our enemies.

[12] When the men heard her voice, they hurried down to the gates and called for the town officials. [13] Everyone, young and old, ran together to the gate. No one could believe that Judith had come back. They opened the gate for her and her slave and welcomed them. Then, when they had lit a fire to give some light and had gathered around the two women, [14] Judith shouted,

Praise God, give him praise! Praise God, who has not held back his mercy from the people of Israel. Tonight he has used me to destroy our enemies. [15] She then took the head out of the food bag and showed it to the people. Here, she said,

is the head of Holofernes, the general of the Assyrian

army, and here is the mosquito net from his bed, where he lay in a drunken stupor. The Lord used a woman to kill him. ¹⁶ As the Lord lives, I swear that Holofernes never touched me, although my beauty deceived him and brought him to his ruin. I was not defiled or disgraced; the Lord took care of me through it all.

¹⁷ Everyone in the city was utterly amazed. They bowed down and worshiped God, praying together,

Our God, you are worthy of great praise. Today you have triumphed over the enemies of your people.

¹⁸ Then Uzziah said,

Judith, my dear, the Most High God has blessed you more than any other woman on earth. How worthy of praise is the Lord God who created heaven and earth! He guided you as you cut off the head of our deadliest enemy. ¹⁹ Your trust in God will never be forgotten by those who tell of God's power. ²⁰ May God give you everlasting honor for what you have done. May he reward you with blessings, because you remained faithful to him and did not hesitate to risk your own life to relieve the oppression of your people.

All the people replied,
Amen, amen!

Judith 14

Judith's Plan

14 Then Judith said to them,

My friends, please follow my advice. In the morning, take this head and hang it on the town wall. ² Appoint a leader for yourselves, and at sunrise have all your able-bodied men take their weapons and march out of the town with him, as if they were going down into the valley to attack the Assyrian outpost.

³ The Assyrian guards will grab their weapons and rush back to camp to wake up their officers. The officers will run to Holofernes' tent but will not find him, and the whole army will be terrified and retreat as you advance against them. ⁴ Then you and all the other Israelites will be able to follow them and kill them as they retreat.

⁵ But before you do any of this, send Achior the Ammonite to me. I want to see if he recognizes Holofernes, the man who spoke of Israel with contempt and sent Achior to us, thinking he would be killed along with the rest of us.

Achior's Conversion

⁶ So they called Achior from Uzziah's house. But when he came and saw the head of Holofernes in the hands of one of the men, Achior fainted and fell to the

floor. [7] When they had helped him up, Achior bowed at Judith's feet in respect.

May every family in the land of Judah praise you, he said,
and may every nation tremble with terror when they hear your name.[8] Please tell me how you managed to do this.

While all the people were gathered around, Judith told him everything that she had done from the day she left the town until that moment.[9] When she had finished her story, the people cheered so loudly that the whole town echoed with sounds of joy.

[10] When Achior heard all that the God of Israel had done, he became a firm believer. He was circumcised and made a member of the Israelite community, as his descendants are to the present day.

Panic in Holofernes' Camp

[11] The next morning the Israelites hung the head of Holofernes on the wall of the town. All of them took up their weapons and went out in companies to the slopes in front of the town. [12] When the Assyrians saw what was happening, they sent word to their officers, and these reported the matter to their superiors. [13] These men then went to Holofernes' tent and said to Bagoas,

Wake up the general! Those worthless Israelites have dared to come down from the mountain to attack us; they are just asking to be destroyed.

14 Bagoas went in and clapped his hands in front of the sleeping quarters of the tent, thinking that Holofernes was in bed with Judith. 15 When there was no answer, he drew the curtain aside and went in, and there he found the headless body sprawled over a footstool.

16 Bagoas let out a yell. He screamed, tore his clothes, and started groaning and weeping. 17 He went into the tent where Judith had stayed, but of course he did not find her. He rushed out and shouted to the officers,

18 They have tricked us! One Israelite woman has disgraced Nebuchadnezzar's whole kingdom. Look in there! Holofernes is lying dead on the ground and his head is gone! 19 When the officers heard this, they tore their clothes in grief; and as the panic spread, wild cries and shouts were heard throughout the camp.

Judith 15

Israel's Victory

15 When the soldiers heard what had happened, they were horrified ² and began to tremble with fear. They all scattered in different directions from the camp, making no effort to stay together as they tried to escape along the paths in the mountains and valleys. ³ The soldiers who had camped in the mountains around Bethulia also began to retreat. Then all the Israelite soldiers came charging down on them.

⁴ Uzziah sent messengers to the towns of Betomesthaim, Bebai, Choba, and Kola, and throughout the land of Israel to tell everyone what had happened and to urge them to join in pursuing and destroying the enemy. ⁵ When they received the message, they all attacked the Assyrians and chased them as far as Choba, slaughtering them as they went.

Even the people of Jerusalem and others living in the mountains joined the attack when the messengers told them what had happened in the Assyrian camp. The people of the regions of Gilead and Galilee blocked the path of the retreating Assyrians and inflicted heavy losses on them. They pursued them as far as the region around Damascus.

⁶ The rest of the people in Bethulia went down to the Assyrian camp, plundered it and carried away enough loot to make themselves very rich. ⁷ When the Israelite soldiers returned from the slaughter, they helped themselves to what was left. There was so much of it that the people of the towns and villages in the hill country also shared in the loot.

Israel Celebrates the Victory

⁸ The High Priest Joakim and the Council of Israel came from Jerusalem to see for themselves what great things the Lord had done for his people and to meet Judith and congratulate her. ⁹ When they arrived, they all praised her,

You are Jerusalem's crowning glory, the heroine of Israel, the pride and joy of our people! ¹⁰ You have won this great victory for Israel by yourself. God, the Almighty, is pleased with what you have done. May he bless you as long as you live.

All the people responded,
Amen.

¹¹ It took the people thirty days to finish looting the camp of the Assyrians. Judith was given Holofernes' tent, all his silver, his bowls, his couches, and all his furniture. She took them and loaded as much as she could on her mule; then she brought her wagons and loaded them too. ¹² All the Israelite women came to see her; they

sang her praises and danced in her honor. On this joyful occasion Judith and the other women waved ivy-covered branches [13] and wore wreaths of olive leaves on their heads. Judith took her place at the head of the procession to lead the women as they danced. All the men of Israel followed, wearing wreaths of flowers on their heads, carrying their weapons, and singing songs of praise.

Judith 16

Judith's Song of Praise

16 Then Judith sang a song of thanksgiving there with all Israel present, and the people joined in this song of praise. ² She sang,

Praise my God and sing to him;

praise the Lord with drums and cymbals;

play a new song for him.

Praise him and call on him for help.

³ The Lord is a warrior who ends war.

He rescued me from my pursuers

and brought me back to his people's camp.

⁴ Down from the mountains of the north came the Assyrians,

with their tens of thousands of soldiers.

Their troops blocked the rivers in the valleys;

their cavalry covered the mountains.

⁵ They threatened to set fire to our country,

slaughter our young men,

dash our babies to the ground,

take our children away as captives,

and carry off all our young women.

⁶ But the Lord Almighty tricked them;

he used a woman to stop them.

⁷ Their hero was not slain by young soldiers

or attacked and killed by mighty giants.

It was Judith, the daughter of Merari,

who brought him down with her beauty.

⁸ She gave victory to the oppressed people of Israel,

when she took off her widow's clothes,

and put on a linen dress to entice him.

She put on her rich perfumes

and tied a ribbon around her hair.

⁹ Her dainty sandal caught his eye;

her beauty captured his heart.

Then the sword slashed through his neck.

¹⁰ The Persians trembled at her daring;

the Medes were amazed at her bravery.

¹¹ Then our people shouted in victory.

They had been weak and oppressed,

but they forced the enemy to retreat in panic and fear.

¹² We are the descendants of slaves,

but our enemies turned and ran;

we killed them like runaway slaves.

They were destroyed by the army of the Lord.

¹³ I will sing a new song to my God.

O Lord, you are strong and glorious!

You have never been defeated.

¹⁴ Let all your creatures serve you.

You gave the command,

and all of them came into being;

you breathed on them,

and all of them were created.

No one can oppose your command.

15 The mountains and the seas tremble,

and rocks melt like wax when you come near.

But there is mercy for all who obey you.

16 The Lord is more pleased with those who obey him

than with all the choice meat on the altar,

or with all the most fragrant sacrifices.

17 The nations who rise up against my people are

doomed.

The Lord Almighty will punish them on Judgment Day.

He will send fire and worms to devour their bodies,

and they will weep in pain forever.

Judith's Fame

18 When the people arrived in Jerusalem, they purified themselves and worshiped God. They presented their burnt offerings, freewill offerings, and gifts. 19 Judith dedicated to God all of Holofernes' property, which the people had given to her. And as a special offering in fulfillment of a vow, she presented to the Lord the mosquito net which she had taken from Holofernes' bed. 20 For three months the people continued to celebrate in front of the Temple in Jerusalem, and Judith

stayed there with them.

21 When the celebrations had ended, everyone returned home, and Judith went back to Bethulia to live on her own estate. For the rest of her life she was famous throughout the land of Israel. 22 Many men wanted to marry her, but she never remarried after the death of her husband Manasseh. 23-24 Her fame continued to spread, and she lived in the house her husband had left her. Before she died, Judith divided her property among her husband's and her own close relatives and set her slave woman free. When she died in Bethulia at the age of 105, she was buried beside her husband, and the people of Israel mourned her death for seven days. 25 As long as Judith lived, and for many years after her death, no one dared to threaten the people of Israel.

New Members/Guests

Sisters Helping Sisters in Christ would like to welcome any new members and invited guests to our ministry. We hope you will make SHSIC your home. May God bless you!

Prayer

Heavenly Father, we thank you for bringing us together today to give you praise. We pray that you will strengthen us today and send us your Holy Spirit to help us serve you better. It is our desire to be the best that we can be, always giving you the Glory for the work you have done and are doing in our lives.

We pray for our loved ones and for all of your children. We pray for all those who are lost and ask that you will send a beacon of light. We know that it is not your desire for any to be lost and we pray that their hearts soften to the Word and they will hear what the Spirit is saying.

In Jesus name we pray, Amen.

Printed in Great Britain
by Amazon

16662901R00037